40

DAYS

—— of ——

HOPE

Books by Paul David Tripp

40 Days of Faith

40 Days of Grace

40 Days of Hope

40 Days of Love

A Quest for More: Living for Something Bigger Than You

Age of Opportunity: A Biblical Guide for Parenting Teens (Resources for Changing Lives)

Awe: Why It Matters for Everything We Think, Say, and Do

Broken-Down House: Living Productively in a World Gone Bad

Come, Let Us Adore Him: A Daily Advent Devotional

Dangerous Calling: Confronting the Unique Challenges of Pastoral Ministry

Forever: Why You Can't Live without It

Grief: Finding Hope Again

How People Change (with Timothy S. Lane)

Instruments in the Redeemer's Hands: People in Need of Change Helping People in Need of Change (Resources for Changing Lives)

Journey to the Cross: A 40-Day Lenten Devotional

Lead: 12 Gospel Principles for Leadership in the Church

Lost in the Middle: Midlife and the Grace of God

My Heart Cries Out: Gospel Meditations for Everyday Life

New Morning Mercies: A Daily Gospel Devotional

Parenting: 14 Gospel Principles That Can Radically Change Your Family

Redeeming Money: How God Reveals and Reorients Our Hearts

Sex in a Broken World: How Christ Redeems What Sin Distorts

Shelter in the Time of Storm: Meditations on God and Trouble

Suffering: Eternity Makes a Difference (Resources for Changing Lives)

Suffering: Gospel Hope When Life Doesn't Make Sense

Teens and Sex: How Should We Teach Them? (Resources for Changing Lives)

War of Words: Getting to the Heart of Your Communication Struggles (Resources for Changing Lives)

What Did You Expect?: Redeeming the Realities of Marriage

Whiter Than Snow: Meditations on Sin and Mercy

40

DAYS

—*of*—

HOPE

PAUL DAVID TRIPP

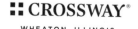

WHEATON, ILLINOIS

40 Days of Hope

Copyright © 2021 by Paul David Tripp

Published by Crossway
   1300 Crescent Street
   Wheaton, Illinois 60187

The devotions in this book appeared previously in Paul David Tripp, *New Morning Mercies: A Daily Gospel Devotional* (Wheaton, IL: Crossway, 2014).

Cover design: Josh Dennis

First printing, 2021

Printed in the United States of America

All Scripture quotations are from the ESV® Bible (The Holy Bible, English Standard Version®), copyright © 2001 by Crossway, a publishing ministry of Good News Publishers. Used by permission. All rights reserved.

All emphases in Scripture quotations have been added by the author.

Trade paperback ISBN: 978-1-4335-7433-7
ePub ISBN: 978-1-4335-7436-8
PDF ISBN: 978-1-4335-7434-4
Mobipocket ISBN: 978-1-4335-7435-1

Library of Congress Cataloging-in-Publication Data

Names: Tripp, Paul David, 1950- author.
Title: 40 days of hope / Paul David Tripp.
Other titles: Forty days of hope
Description: Wheaton, Illinois: Crossway, 2021. | "The devotions in this book appeared previously in Paul David Tripp, *New Morning Mercies: A Daily Gospel Devotional* (Wheaton, IL: Crossway, 2014)."
Identifiers: LCCN 2020038476 (print) | LCCN 2020038477 (ebook) | ISBN 9781433574337 (trade paperback) | ISBN 9781433574344 (pdf) | ISBN 9781433574351 (mobipcket) | ISBN 9781433574368 (epub)
Subjects: LCSH: Hope—Religious aspects—Christianity—Meditations.
Classification: LCC BV4638 .T75 2021 (print) | LCC BV4638 (ebook) | DDC 242/.2—dc23
LC record available at https://lccn.loc.gov/2020038476
LC ebook record available at https://lccn.loc.gov/2020038477

Crossway is a publishing ministry of Good News Publishers.

LB   29 28 27 26 25 24 23 22 21
14 13 12 11 10 9 8 7 6 5 4 3 2 1

INTRODUCTION

PROBABLY FEW DAYS go by without you using the word *hope*.

"I hope we're on time."

"I hope it doesn't rain."

"I hope it's not cancer."

"I hope she'll understand."

"I hope he'll be OK."

"I hope he isn't angry."

"I hope God hears this."

"I hope he loves me."

From the smallest of things to the grandest of concerns, our lives are shaped, directed, motivated, and frustrated by hope. Everyone hopes. Everyone hooks their hope to something or someone. Everyone hopes their hope will come through for them. No one ever purposely hopes in what is hopeless. Everyone longs for hope that is sure. Everyone gets up in the morning motivated by hope of some kind or paralyzed by hopelessness of some kind. For all of us, hoping is so natural and frequent that we lose sight of how significant it is in shaping what we do, how we do it, and how we feel in the process. Yet even though it's natural and we do it all the time, hope is painfully elusive for many of us.

It's important to understand what hope is. Hope always has three elements:

- Desire
- Object
- Expectation

Hope is always fueled by some form of *desire*. It may be the desire to be loved, to be cared for, to be protected, to be understood, to be provided for, to be accepted, to experience comfort or pleasure, to have control, to be forgiven—the list could go on and on. Also, hope always has an *object*. I look to someone or something to satisfy my desire. Lastly, hope carries an *expectation* of when, how, and where the person or thing in which I have placed my hope will deliver what I have hoped for. Almost every day, you entrust your smallest and largest longings into the hands of something or someone with the hope that your longing will be satisfied. To be human is to hope.

The language and drama of hope is splashed all over the pages of Scripture. The Bible is a narrative of hope shattered and hope restored, and in telling its hope story, the Bible speaks to each of the three elements of hope. Scripture has much to say about our longings, that is, the desires that animate us and shape our lives. It tells us what to love and what to hate, what to desire and what to forsake, and what is good for us and what will harm us. Much of the drama of hope in our lives is not that we don't get what we hope for, but that we spend so much of our time hoping for the wrong things.

The Bible has much to say about the object of our hope. It reminds us that when it comes to hope, there are only two places to look. You can look to created things to satisfy the longings of your heart or you can look to the Creator. It really is true that when it comes to fundamental human hope, each of us looks horizontally or vertically. The Bible warns us that if our hope disappoints us, it's because our hope rests on the wrong object. There is only one place to look for hope that is secure, no matter what. Consider these verses:

You are my hiding place and my shield; I hope in your word. (Ps. 119:114)

O Israel, hope in the LORD! For with the LORD there is steadfast love, and with him is plentiful redemption. (Ps. 130:7)

The LORD takes pleasure in those who fear him, in those who hope in his steadfast love. (Ps. 147:11)

For I know the plans I have for you, declares the LORD, plans for welfare and not for evil, to give you a future and a hope. (Jer. 29:11)

"The LORD is my portion," says my soul, "therefore I will hope in him" (Lam. 3:24)

Hope does not put us to shame, because God's love has been poured into our hearts through the Holy Spirit who has been given to us. (Rom. 5:5)

May the God of hope fill you with all joy and peace in believing, so that by the power of the Holy Spirit you may abound in hope. (Rom. 15:13)

Having the eyes of your hearts enlightened, that you may know what is the hope to which he has called you, what are the riches of his glorious inheritance in the saints. (Eph. 1:18)

To them God chose to make known how great among the Gentiles are the riches of the glory of this mystery, which is Christ in you, the hope of glory. (Col. 1:27)

In hope of eternal life, which God, who never lies, promised before the ages began. (Titus 1:2)

Notice what each of these verses does. Each confronts us with the radical, life-reshaping truth that ultimately, true, lasting, and secure hope is a person—the Lord Almighty. Hope—the kind that transforms your life, gives rest to your heart, and ignites new ways of living—is attached to him. Scripture repeatedly invites us, commands us, and implores us to hope in the Lord, and it gives us reason after reason to do so.

Finally, Scripture speaks to our expectations. It promises us that when we hope in the Lord, we will not be disappointed. No, God won't submit to our time expectations, and he won't always deliver what we hope for in the way we expect, but God is powerful, caring, and faithful. He will give us everything he has promised us, and he will generously provide what is best for us. So we wait with patient expectation, knowing that our hope is firm when we hope in the Lord.

It's wonderful to have hope that doesn't rise or fall with changing circumstances. It's a sweet thing to have hope that doesn't die when trouble comes. It's good to be free from placing our hope in things that have no power whatsoever to deliver what we long for. And it's wise to spend time examining what we hope for, reorienting our hope and meditating on the one who alone is a worthy object of our hope.

May this devotional renew your hope, and in renewing your hope, renew your courage, perseverance, and joy.

DAY 1

Hope is not a thing, not a location, not a situation, not an experience. Hope is a person, and his name is Jesus.

IF YOU PAY ATTENTION AND listen carefully to what you and the people around you are saying, you will realize that we are hope obsessed. Day after day, the things we do are fueled by hope. Little third-grader Sally says to her mom as she gets ready for school, "I sure hope the girls at school like me." Mom thinks to herself that day, "I hope our marriage gets better." Teenager Tim says to his buddy, "I got a new job after school; I hope it's decent." Dad worries in the hope that he won't be one of the guys who's caught in the downsizing that his corporation is doing. From hoping that a certain meal will be good to hoping that we will have the moral strength to do the things we should do, our lives are fueled and directed by hope.

What we're all searching for is hope that won't disappoint us, that won't leave us hopeless in the end. And we all want to convince ourselves that what we have placed our hope in will deliver. What are you asking of something when you place your hope in it? You're asking it to give you peace of heart. You're asking it to give your life meaning. You're asking it to give you purpose and direction. You're asking it to give you a reason to continue. You're asking it to help you get through difficulty and disappointment. You're asking it to free you from envy or anxiety. You're asking it to give you joy in the morning and rest at night. Now, that's a lot to ask of anything. That fact confronts you with this reality—if your hope disappoints you, it's because it's the wrong hope.

Romans 5:1–5 talks about a hope that won't disappoint you even in times of suffering. Maybe you're thinking, "Where can I find that hope?" Sturdy hope that does not vanish with the constant changes in situations, locations, and relationships that make up all of our lives—hope that simply will never, ever disappoint us—can be found in only one place. It is not to be found in a certain thing. It is, in fact, a person, Jesus. Whether you have realized it or not, he is what your hoping heart has been searching for, because what you've really been searching for is life, real heart-changing, heart-satisfying life—life to the fullest, life abundant. People can love and respect you, but they can't give you life. Situations can make your life easier, but they can't give you life. Locations can bring some changes to your life, but they can't give you life. Achievements can be temporarily satisfying, but they can't give you life. True lasting hope is never found horizontally. It's only ever found vertically, at the feet of the Messiah, the one who *is* hope. Place your hopeful heart in his hands today. *This has been my prayer for a few months*

FOR FURTHER STUDY AND ENCOURAGEMENT
Colossians 1:15–29

DAY 2

*Every human being places his hope in something,
and every human being asks that hope to deliver
something. Where have you placed your hope?*

WE'VE ALL BEEN HARDWIRED for hope. We all project our lives
out into the future to imagine things as we would like them
to be. We all carry around with us personal hopes and dreams.
We all surrender our hearts to some kind of expectation. We all
silently wish that things could be different than they are. We all
hope *in* something and we all hope *for* something. So much of
how we look at life and how we live our lives is connected to the
things in which we place the fundamental hopes of our lives.

Hope always has three elements—an assessment, an object,
and an expectation. First, hope looks around and assesses that
something or someone could be better than it is; that that
something or someone is somehow broken. If things were as
perfect as they could be, you wouldn't need to hope. Second,
hope always has an object. It is the thing that you bank your
hope on. You ask the object of your hope to fix what is broken
or to deliver what is desired or needed. Third, hope has an
expectation. This is what you ask the object of your hope to
give you, what you hope the object of your hope will deliver.

Now, there are really only two places to look for foundational
life hope, that is, basic meaning and purpose, motivation to
continue, a sense of well-being, and that knowledge that you've
hooked yourself to what life is really all about. You can search

for hope horizontally in the situations, experiences, physical possessions, locations, and relationships of everyday life. There are two problems with looking horizontally. First, all of these things suffer from some degree of brokenness. They are part of the problem, and because they are, they are unable to deliver what you're seeking. Also, these things were never made to be the source of your hope, but to be fingers that point you to where your hope can be found.

Paul says it all in Romans 5:5 when he tells us that hope in God will never put us to shame. It will never embarrass us by failing to deliver. In those words, Paul tells us where hope can be found. It is found only vertically. Only when God is your hope is your hope sure and secure. Only he is able to give you the life that your heart seeks. Only he is able to give your soul the rest that it needs. Only he can deliver the internal peace that is the hunger of every human being. It's only when grace has hooked you to him that you are connected to what life is really all about. In his brief words, Paul confronts us with this thought—if your hope disappoints you, it's because it's the wrong hope! Today, what carries your hope?

FOR FURTHER STUDY AND ENCOURAGEMENT

Job 1

DAY 3

Hope for the believer is not a dream of what could be, but a confident expectation of a guaranteed result that shapes his life.

WE CONSTANTLY SPEAK IN hope language:

- "I hope my company does well."
- "I hope he isn't mad at me."
- "I hope God really does answer prayer."
- "I sure hope it doesn't rain tomorrow."
- "I hope this sickness isn't something serious."

If you are a human being, you hope. You attach your security, your sense of peace and rest to something every day. The question is not whether you hope, but what holds your hope. Take a moment to think about hope with me:

You hope in something. You could argue that the life of a human being is propelled by hope. From the little momentary hope of the young child for food or a toy to the profound hope of the young adult for meaning and purpose, we all hope. We all place our hope in someone or something, and we ask that person or that thing to deliver something to us. What are you placing your hope in right now?

Hope is a lifestyle. Your hope shapes the way you live. Your hope causes you to make the decisions that you make. A lack of hope causes you to feel stuck and de-motivated. Confident hope makes you decisive and courageous. Wobbly hope makes

14

you timid and indecisive. Hope is not just something you do with your brain. You always live your hope in some way.

Most of our hopes disappoint us. We all do it. We place our hope in things in this fallen world that simply can't deliver. Your spouse can't make you happy. Your job won't make you content. Your possessions can't satisfy your heart. Your physical health won't give you inner peace. Your friends can't give you meaning and purpose. When our hopes disappoint us, it is a sign that we've put our hopes in the wrong things.

There are only two places to look for hope. The theology of hope is quite simple. There are only two places to put your hope. You rest the hope of your life in the hands of the Creator or you look to the creation for hope.

Hope in God is sure hope. When you hope in the Lord, you not only hope in the one who created and controls the universe, but also in one who is glorious in grace and abounding in love. Now, that's hope that is well placed and will never disappoint.

FOR FURTHER STUDY AND ENCOURAGEMENT
Psalm 40

DAY 4

*Hope is more than wishing things will work
out. It is resting in the God who holds all
things in his wise and powerful hands.*

AS I NOTED EARLIER, we use the word *hope* in a variety of ways. Sometimes it connotes a wish about something over which we have no control at all. We say, "I sure hope the train comes soon," or, "I hope it doesn't rain on the day of the picnic." These are wishes for things, but we wouldn't bank on them. The word *hope* also depicts what we think should happen. We say, "I hope he will choose to be honest this time," or, "I hope the judge brings down a guilty verdict." Here hope reveals an internal sense of morality or justice. We also use *hope* in a motivational sense. We say, "I did this in the hope that it would pay off in the end," or, "I got married in the hope that he would treat me in marriage the way he treated me in courtship." All of this is to say that because the word *hope* is used in a variety of ways, it is important for us to understand how this word is used in Scripture or in its gospel sense.

Biblical hope is foundationally more than a faint wish for something. Biblical hope is deeper than moral expectation, although it includes that. Biblical hope is more than a motivation for a choice or action, although it is that as well. So what is biblical hope? It is a confident expectation of a guaranteed result that changes the way you live. Let's pull this definition apart.

First, biblical hope is confident. It is confident because it is not based on your wisdom, faithfulness, or power, but on the awesome power, love, faithfulness, grace, patience, and wisdom of God. Because God is who he is and will never, ever change, hope in him is hope well placed and secure.

Hope is also an expectation of a guaranteed result. It is being sure that God will do all that he has planned and promised to do. You see, his promises are only as good as the extent of his rule, but since he rules everything everywhere, I know that resting in the promises of his grace will never leave me empty and embarrassed. I may not understand what is happening and I may not know what is coming around the corner, but I know that God does and that he controls it all. So even when I am confused, I can have hope, because my hope does not rest on my understanding, but on God's goodness and his rule.

Finally, true hope changes the way you live. When you have hope that is guaranteed, you live with confidence and courage that you would otherwise not have. That confidence and courage cause you to make choices of faith that would seem foolish to someone who does not have your hope. If you're God's child, you never have to live hopelessly, because hope has invaded your life by grace, and his name is Jesus!

FOR FURTHER STUDY AND ENCOURAGEMENT
Psalm 20

DAY 5

Never forget that what God required, you couldn't do. Christ did it for you. His grace is your hope.

IN SOME WAY, IT IS true of us all. We want to swindle ourselves into thinking that we are righteous enough to be accepted in the eyes of God. Maybe for you it is:

- "Look at how much I give to charity."
- "Look at how hospitable I am."
- "Look at the level of my theological knowledge."
- "Look at how often I share the gospel with others."
- "Look at what a good marriage I have."
- "Look how successful my business is."
- "Look at how I've resisted pornography or adultery."
- "Look at the fact that I homeschool my children."
- "Look at how I never curse or swear."
- "Look at how many short-term mission trips I've been on."
- "Look at how consistent my personal devotions are."
- "Look at my willingness to lead a small group."

You and I tend to want to point to anything we can to prove that we are not lawbreakers, but law keepers. Yet the whole argument of the Bible is that if we were able to keep the law with perfection and consistency, Jesus would not have had to come. The sad reality is that alone, none of us is righteous. None of us measures up. None of us has any power whatsoever to keep the law so consistently as to achieve acceptance by a completely holy God. So it was essential that Jesus would come and live in a way that none of us could ever live, to die the death that we all deserve to die, and to rise, defeating sin and death. Hope is never to be found in your performance, no matter what actions you are able to point to. Sin is your infection, and without the grace of the Lord Jesus Christ, it is also your demise. It is inescapable and morally debilitating, and it will lead to your death.

So abandon hope in your own righteousness. Abandon the delusion that somehow you can measure up. Run to the place where hope can be found and throw yourself again today on the grace of Jesus. He did what you could never do so that you would be welcomed into the arms of a righteous God and be fully accepted even though, in reality, you are anything but righteous. How can God accept you and not compromise his own righteousness? He can do this because Christ's righteousness has been credited to your moral account. Now, that's amazing grace!

FOR FURTHER STUDY AND ENCOURAGEMENT
Hebrews 2:10–18

DAY 6

*The cross of Jesus Christ stands as a beacon
of hope in a world gone bad. Life, hope,
forgiveness, and change really are possible!*

THE CROSS DOESN'T STAND STAINED with the death blood of
the Messiah in the darkness of moral defeat. It is not the sad
symbol of a plan gone wrong. It doesn't preach that the good
gets smashed at evil's hand. It doesn't suck salvation hope out
of those who would believe. The cross isn't the grand symbol
of redemption's embarrassment. The cross shouldn't make you
ashamed. No, it should stand at the epicenter of your boasting.
Hear the words of the apostle Paul: "But far be it from me to
boast except in the cross of our Lord Jesus Christ, by which
the world has been crucified to me, and I to the world" (Gal.
6:14). In a sin-scarred world, there really aren't many things
worth boasting about. As sinners, rescued from ourselves by
powerful grace, we don't have many valid reasons for puff-
ing out our chests. We're all more case studies of mercy than
heroes. The world around us groans under the weight of its
fallenness. The history of humanity would be a sick and dreary
story if it weren't for the rough-hewn tree of death on the hill
of Golgotha. It was an unlikely place for a scene of history-
changing triumph. The place where they executed criminals
seems to be the last place to go to find hope. The scene where
they killed the world's only innocent man doesn't seem to be a
place that excites celebration. But such is the paradox of grace.

Death is the doorway to life. Hopelessness is the entrance to hope. Weakness is the place to find strength. Injustice is where mercy flows. Life comes to those who deserve death. Defeat is actually a victory. The end is really a beginning. Out of sorrow comes eternal celebration. The tomb is the place where new life begins.

The impossible paradoxes of redemption become the regular moves of transforming grace. Hope is sung to suffering's tune. Life is played on death's instruments. Grace doesn't play by the law's score. God composes hope from tragedy's notes. So we look at Calvary and we don't sing a dirge—we sing a song of triumph and celebration, of hope and salvation. Satan's players have not been able to drown out salvation's song. The songs of hope by the company of the redeemed will never end. They grow in volume, celebration, and glory. The cross is the subject of those songs, and its life-giving mercy is the chorus.

It is the cross of Jesus Christ that gives you reason to hope, sing, celebrate, and live. It was never the interruption of God's saving plan, but the essential means of it. It was never a defeat. It was always a victory.

FOR FURTHER STUDY AND ENCOURAGEMENT
Revelation 5

DAY 7

*The cross is evidence that in the hands of the
Redeemer, moments of apparent defeat become
wonderful moments of grace and victory.*

AT THE CENTER OF A BIBLICAL worldview is this radical recognition—the most horrible thing that ever happened was the most wonderful thing that ever happened. Consider the cross of Jesus Christ. Could it be possible for something to happen that was more terrible than this? Could any injustice be greater? Could any loss be more painful? Could any suffering be worse? The only man who ever lived a life that was perfect in every way possible, who gave his life for the sake of many, and who willingly suffered from birth to death in loyalty to his calling was cruelly and publicly murdered in the most vicious of ways. How could it happen that the Son of Man could die? How could it be that men could capture and torture the Messiah? Was this not the end of everything good, true, and beautiful? If this could happen, is there any hope for the world?

Well, the answer is yes. There is hope! The cross was not the end of the story! In God's righteous and wise plan, this dark and disastrous moment was ordained to be the moment that would fix all the dark and disastrous things that sin had done to the world. This moment of death was at the same time a moment of life. This hopeless moment was the moment when eternal hope was given. This terrible moment of injustice was at the very same time a moment of amazing grace. This moment of extreme suffering guaranteed that suffering would end one day, once and for all. This moment of sadness welcomed us to eternal joy of heart and life. The capture and death of Christ purchased for us life and freedom. The very worst thing that could happen was, at the very same time, the very best thing that could happen. Only God is able to do such a thing.

The same God who planned that the worst thing would be the best thing is your Father. He rules over every moment in your life, and in powerful grace he is able to do for you just what he did in redemptive history. He takes the disasters in your life and makes them tools of redemption. He takes your failure and employs it as a tool of grace. He uses the "death" of the fallen world to motivate you to reach out for life. The hardest things in your life become the sweetest tools of grace in his wise and loving hands.

So be careful how you make sense of your life. What looks like a disaster may in fact be grace. What looks like the end may be the beginning. What looks hopeless may be God's instrument to give you real and lasting hope. Your Father is committed to taking what seems so bad and turning it into something that is very, very good.

FOR FURTHER STUDY AND ENCOURAGEMENT
Acts 2:14–36

DAY 8

We are fearful. God's presence gives courage.
We are alienated. His love draws us near. We
are doubtful. His promises give us hope.

GOD MEETS US WHERE WE ARE. This is the beautiful, hope-giving reality of grace. If God asked us to meet him where he is, we would all be damned. There is no better example of this than Jesus's response to Peter after Peter's denial:

When they had finished breakfast, Jesus said to Simon Peter, "Simon, son of John, do you love me more than these?" He said to him, "Yes, Lord; you know that I love you." He said to him, "Feed my lambs." He said to him a second time, "Simon, son of John, do you love me?" He said to him, "Yes, Lord; you know that I love you." He said to him, "Tend my sheep." He said to him the third time, "Simon, son of John, do you love me?" Peter was grieved because he said to him the third time, "Do you love me?" and he said to him, "Lord, you know everything; you know that I love you." Jesus said to him, "Feed my sheep. Truly, truly, I say to you, when you were young, you used to dress yourself and walk wherever you wanted, but when you are old, you will stretch out your hands, and another will dress you and carry you where you do not want to go." (This he said to show by what kind of death he was to glorify God.) And after saying this he said to him, "Follow me." (John 21:15–19)

If there's someone on whom you would expect Jesus to turn his back forever, it would be Peter. How could he deny Jesus, even after being warned? Wasn't that unforgivable? No! What Peter did was not a picture of the defeat of the cross. The opposite is true. Peter's denial is a shockingly concrete picture of the essentiality of the cross of Jesus Christ. The life, death, and resurrection of Jesus were necessary because we are people like Peter. We have no power in ourselves to be faithful, wise, good, and righteous. We cannot save ourselves. We are people in need of rescue. Without the rescue of grace, we are a danger to ourselves and to others, without hope and without God.

So in amazing condescending grace, God meets us where we are, just as he did with Peter. He comes to us in our fear. He draws near to us when we are separated. He meets us in our doubt. He pursues us when we wander. When we sin, he comes to us with conviction and forgiveness. He empowers us when we're weak. He restores us when we are unfaithful. When we deny him, he does not deny us. He comes to us at the moment of our salvation, and he comes to us again and again as we journey from the "already" to the "not yet." He sits down with us, assuring us again of his love, drawing out from us love for him, and sending us on our way to do the work he has chosen us to do. He does not wait for us to come to him; he comes to us. It is the way of grace.

FOR FURTHER STUDY AND ENCOURAGEMENT
John 18:15–18

DAY 9

*Because God rules all the places where you live,
he is able to deliver his promises to you in the
very circumstances where they are needed.*

I DON'T KNOW WHETHER YOU have ever thought of this before,
but God's promises are only as good as the extent of his sovereignty. He can deliver what you need only in the places where
he rules. If his rule is not firm and unchanging, his promises
are not either. I think that many of us fail to make this connection, and when we do, we allow ourselves to celebrate his
promises while subtly resisting his rule. He is your sovereign
Savior. If he were not sovereign, you would have no guarantee
that he could exercise the authority necessary to be your Savior.

Think for a moment about the flow of biblical history. Think
of the many generations of people that existed between the fall
of Adam and Eve and the birth of Jesus Christ. Think of the
myriad situations and locations in that span of time. Think
of all the human governments that rose and fell. Think of all
the decisions, great and small, that people made. Think of the
constant life-and-death cycle of the physical creation. Now
consider this—in order for Jesus to be born as was promised,
to live as was necessary, and to die and rise on our behalf as
he said he would, God had to exercise absolute rule over the
forces of nature and complete control over the events of human
history so that, at just the right moment, Jesus would be born,
live, die, and rise again for our redemption.

Without the rule of the Almighty, there would've been no prophets predicting the birth of the Messiah, no angels announcing it to the shepherds, and no Mary wondering about the babe in the manger. There would've been no miracles in Palestine. There would've been no perfectly obedient Son of Man. There would've been no unjust trial and cruel cross. There would've been no disciples to pass the life-giving gospel down to us, no Scripture, no church, and no hope of eternal life.

If you are going to reach for the life-giving promises of the gospel, you must also celebrate the absolute rule of the one who, because of his rule, is able to deliver those promises to you. Hope is not found just in the beauty of those promises, but in the incalculable power and authority of the one who has made them. There is no hope in the promises of one who has little power over the situations and locations where they must be delivered. But you can have hope because your Lord has complete rule over all the places where you will need his promises to become your reality.

FOR FURTHER STUDY AND ENCOURAGEMENT
Jeremiah 32:16–27

DAY 10

*Your hope is not in your ability to love God, but
in his unrelenting and unshakable love for you.*

THERE IS NOTHING THAT ARGUES more for our desperate need
for grace than the two greatest commandments: that we love
God and love other people (Matt. 22:34–40). The call to love
exposes how dark and depraved our hearts really are. Let's be
honest here. It doesn't take much for us to be irritated with
other people. It doesn't take much for us to become impatient.
Little interruptions, disagreements, and obstacles can cause
us to well up with anger. We are easily dismissive of others.
It's too easy for us to be prejudiced and judgmental. It's far
too simple for us to be racist and xenophobic. In a variety of
ways, we look down on others, failing to see them with eyes
of compassion and hearts of mercy. It's so easy for us to judge
others as foolish, lazy, or otherwise incompetent. I know I'm
not the only one who struggles with these things. I think if
we were willing to look at our hearts in the mirror of the word
of God, we would be shocked at how unnatural love is for us.
But if horizontal love is hard for us, vertical love is even
harder. The connection between the two is cogently made
in 1 John 4:20: "If anyone says, 'I love God,' and hates his
brother, he is a liar; for he who does not love his brother whom
he has seen cannot love God whom he has not seen." Wow!
There it is. If I have such a struggle loving the people around
me, how great and deep must be my struggle to love God? It's

one thing to acknowledge God's existence; it's one thing to mentally assent to the truths of his word; and it's one thing to participate in the formal ministry of his church. But it is an entirely different thing to have every aspect of my life shaped and moved by love for him.

Yes, the power of sin has been broken by the work of Jesus, but the presence of sin still remains and is being progressively eradicated. So there is still sin in our hearts. That means our hearts are still fickle, we still rebel and want our own way, we still forget God and his glory, we still write our own rules, we still love our kingdoms more than we love his, we still demand what we don't deserve, and we still question God's goodness when we don't get our own way. We all fall into doing these things because we just do not love God as we should. We tend to love ourselves and we tend to love the world, but very often the love of the Father simply is not in us.

So your hope in life and death is never to be found in the degree of your love for God. It is only ever found in the magnitude of his love for you. This love is yours as a gift of his grace even on those days where your heart has run after other lovers. That's just how beautiful and faithful his love for you really is.

FOR FURTHER STUDY AND ENCOURAGEMENT
1 John 4:10–21

DAY 11

Today you have hope, not because people like
you or because situations are easy, but because
God has placed his unshakable love on you.

LOOKING TO THE FALLEN WORLD to give you hope to continue just doesn't work very well. Think about the address where you live:

- You live with fallen people who inevitably disappoint you in some way.
- You live in a broken world where corruption and injustice are commonplace.
- You face temptation somehow, some way every day.
- Your physical body is growing older and can be infected with disease.
- Storms and pollution complicate your life.
- Satan prowls, doing his evil work.
- The physical creation groans, waiting for redemption.
- War and strife pit nation against nation.
- Partiality and prejudice divide us.

Sin creates constant instability and unpredictability around us because the world that we live in simply does not function the way the one who created it intended. There are times when life works well and seems easy, but there are many other times when sickness, a betrayal, an injustice, a financial loss, the corruption of an official, a crime against you, or the death of a loved one makes life very hard.

It is so good to know that you don't have to frantically look for sturdy hope horizontally, where it just can't be found. No, you are freed from this search because powerful grace has connected you to hope. You see, hope is not a situation, a location, a feeling, or a relationship. As we saw earlier, hope is a person, and his name is Jesus. He died so that you can know life, real life. He is present with you so that you are guaranteed to have everything you need. He forgives you of all your sins and empowers you to do much better. He never leaves you or turns his back on you. He always responds to you in tender compassion and righteous justice. He never mocks your weaknesses or throws your sin in your face. He never gets tired of you or gives up on his relationship with you. He doesn't ask you to earn what you can never deserve, and he never makes you feel guilty for needing his good gifts. His love isn't conditional and his grace is never temporary. Jesus is your hope as you live in a world where hope is a precious and rare commodity. And remember, you are connected to him forever. This means there will be a day when you won't have to hope anymore, because the paradise you have hoped for will be the eternal reality in which you live.

FOR FURTHER STUDY AND ENCOURAGEMENT
Psalm 42

DAY 12

*We panic. God stays true to his sovereign plan. We
wonder. God knows the end from the beginning.
We pray. God answers with wisdom and grace.*

THERE SIMPLY IS NO PANIC in heaven. God is never anxious.
There is no confusion in the Trinity. God never wrings his hands
and wishes he had made a better choice. God never worries
about what is going to happen next or stresses over how things
are going to turn out. God is never surprised or caught up short.
He is never in a situation that overwhelms him. God never feels
needy or unprepared. God never regrets that he did not do better.
God never fails at a task. He never makes promises that he cannot keep. He never forgets what he said or what he wants to do
next. God never contradicts himself or fails to be exactly who he
said he was. He is all-powerful, absolutely perfect in every way,
faithful to every word, sovereign over all that is, the definition
of love, and he is righteous, just, tender, and patient all at the
same time. He is not dismayed or distracted by our panic and
our questions. No, the sovereign move of his grace marches on!

> Blessed be the God and Father of our Lord Jesus Christ,
> who has blessed us in Christ with every spiritual blessing
> in the heavenly places, even as he chose us in him before
> the foundation of the world, that we should be holy and
> blameless before him. In love he predestined us for adoption
> as sons through Jesus Christ, according to the purpose of

his will, to the praise of his glorious grace, with which he has blessed us in the Beloved. In him we have redemption through his blood, the forgiveness of our trespasses, according to the riches of his grace, which he lavished upon us, in all wisdom and insight making known to us the mystery of his will, according to his purpose, which he set forth in Christ as a plan for the fullness of time, to unite all things in him, things in heaven and things on earth.

In him we have obtained an inheritance, having been predestined according to the purpose of him who works all things according to the counsel of his will, so that we who were the first to hope in Christ might be to the praise of his glory. (Eph. 1:3–12)

So God is not discouraged in the face of our weakness and wondering. His plan is not thwarted by our spiritual vacillation. He doesn't look at us and ask whether it's worth it. No, in the face of our ongoing struggles, his plan marches on. Why? It marches on because it is not based on our character, but on his. Redemption does not rest on our resolve, but on his. Salvation doesn't hang on our strength, but on his. We have hope because it all comes from him and rests on him. It is humbling to admit, but it is the only place of hope. Nothing of our salvation depends on us. It all rests on his sovereign grace. Here is the bottom line: he is able, he is willing, and he is faithful. Grace supplies everything we need. Grace will win!

FOR FURTHER STUDY AND ENCOURAGEMENT

Philippians 4:19–20

DAY 13

*God justifies the ungodly. This means there
really is hope for people like us.*

I WISH I COULD SAY THAT all my actions are godly, but they're
not. I wish I could say that I always live with God's kingdom
in view, but I don't. I wish I could say that all my responses
to the people in my life are motivated by love for God and
for them, but they're not. I wish awe of God was the principal
motivation for all I do, but often it isn't. I wish I could say
that I love God's glory more than my own, but there are still
moments when I live as a glory thief. I wish I could say that
selfishness and greed are in my rearview mirror, but there's
evidence that they're not. I wish I could say that I have a heart
of pure submission, but, sadly, there are times when I want my
own way. I wish I could say that I always exhibit the fruit of the
Spirit, but there are times when I don't. I wish I could say that
I always live inside the wisdom boundaries of God's word, but
there are times when I foolishly think I'm smarter than God.

I wish I could say that materialism doesn't kidnap my heart
anymore, but there are still times when it does. I wish I could
say that I always rest in God's control, but there are times when
I want to be in charge. I wish I could say that there are never
times when I am irritated or impatient, but I still struggle with
both on occasion. I wish I could say that the worship of God
rules my heart unchallenged, but the truth is that idolatry still
nips at me. I wish I could say that I always rest in the righteous-

ness of Christ, but there are still times when I give way to the pride of parading my so-called righteousness before others. I wish I could say that the great spiritual battle is over for me, but there is clear and regular evidence that it is not.

All this means that I value justifying grace. I celebrate that, in Christ, God found a way to be "just and the justifier" (Rom. 3:26) of the ungodly. I am daily thankful for the perfect life of Jesus. I am thankful that he subjected himself to the temptations of this fallen world. I am thankful that on the cross he took my stripes and carried my guilt and shame. I am thankful that he took the father's rejection. I am thankful that he burst out of that tomb, conquering death. I am thankful that his righteousness is attributed to my account. I am thankful that he fulfilled the law and satisfied the Father's anger. I still celebrate the fact that I have been granted full, complete, and unending acceptance.

I celebrate justifying grace because I am still unable to stand before God based on my own righteousness. I still fall short of his glory. So I am so very thankful that justifying grace ensures that I will forever be accepted as one of his righteous ones, even though I still don't measure up. Yes, today I have reason again to be thankful for justifying grace.

FOR FURTHER STUDY AND ENCOURAGEMENT
Galatians 5:4–5

DAY 14

*If you are not fully formed into the image
of Jesus, your Redeemer is neither satisfied nor
finished, and neither should you be.*

WE DON'T TALK ABOUT it much. It doesn't find its way into our theological outlines. It's not the typical way we think about our Redeemer. Yet it is an observation that not only gives you hope, but defines for you what your Lord is doing right here, right now. Here it is—you serve a dissatisfied Redeemer. You ought to be very thankful that your Lord isn't easily satisfied. He does not do his work poorly or incompletely. He does not walk away from what he has begun until it is perfectly finished. He does not grow bored, tired, discouraged, or distracted. He does not have a short attention span. He does not suffer from redemptive attention deficit disorder. He never grows impatient. He isn't irritated by how long his work is taking. He never wishes that he hadn't begun in the first place. He never tries to rush what takes time. He never uses his power to turn what must be a process into an event. He never wonders if it's worth it and contemplates calling it all off.

Your Redeemer is zealous for one goal—the final renewal of all things. Ultimate salvation from all that sin is and all that sin has broken is his unrelenting pursuit. He will continue to unleash his power to accomplish redemption and he will not be satisfied until the last enemy is under his feet and the final kingdom has come. Yes, there is great and eternal hope for you in the dissatisfaction of your Redeemer.

Our problem is that we are all too easily satisfied. We're satisfied with a little bit of theological knowledge, a degree of biblical literacy, occasional moments of ministry, and a measure of personal spiritual growth. We're sadly satisfied with being a little bit better when God's goal is that we be completely remolded into his image. In fact, it is even worse than that. Not only are we too easily satisfied, willing to stop before the Redeemer's work is fully accomplished in us, we are all very easily distracted. We get distracted by the temporary glories of the created world, and we actually begin to think that we can find our satisfaction there. So we quit pressing on because our Redeemer is pressing on. While he, in glorious dissatisfaction, still works to redeem us from us, we are out chasing other lovers. We begin to believe that they can do for us what he alone can do. We begin to invest our time, energy, and hope in things that can never deliver.

Hope is not found in the places where our hearts look for satisfaction, but in the dissatisfaction of our Redeemer. He will complete his work even in those moments when we don't care that he does.

FOR FURTHER STUDY AND ENCOURAGEMENT
1 Thessalonians 5:23–24

DAY 15

*God's care is sure, but will you run to him in your
time of need or look elsewhere for hope and comfort?*

BY HIS PROMISES, God invites us to run to him:

- "[Cast] all your anxieties on him, because he cares for you" (1 Pet. 5:7).
- "He has said, 'I will never leave you nor forsake you'" (Heb. 13:5).
- "Come to me, all who labor and are heavy laden, and I will give you rest. Take my yoke upon you, and learn from me, for I am gentle and lowly in heart, and you will find rest for your souls. For my yoke is easy, and my burden is light" (Matt. 11:28–30).
- "The LORD is my light and my salvation; whom shall I fear? The LORD is the stronghold of my life; of whom shall I be afraid?" (Ps. 27:1).
- "He gives power to the faint, and to him who has no might he increases strength. Even youths shall faint and be weary, and young men shall fall exhausted; but they who wait for the LORD shall renew their strength; they shall mount up with wings like eagles; they shall run and not be weary; they shall walk and not faint" (Isa. 40:29–31).
- "And my God will supply every need of yours according to his riches in glory in Christ Jesus" (Phil. 4:19).
- "Cast your burden on the LORD, and he will sustain you; he will never permit the righteous to be moved" (Ps. 55:22).

These are just a small representation of God's words of invitation and welcome. He really is the "Father of mercies and God of all comfort" (2 Cor. 1:3). He can do for you what no one else can do. He has power that no one else possesses. He is able and willing to meet you in your moments of need, even when that need is self-inflicted. He will never mock you in your weakness. He will not stand idly by and sarcastically say, "I told you so." He finds no joy in your suffering. He is full of compassion. He abounds in mercy. He will never walk away disgusted. He will never use your weakness against you. He has no favorites and shows no partiality. He never grows tired. He never becomes impatient. He will never quit because he's had enough. He will never refuse to give you what he's promised because you've messed up so badly. He is just as faithful to all of his promises on your very worst day as he is on your very best day. He doesn't ask you to earn his compassion or to do things to gain his mercy. He knows how weak and fickle your heart is, yet he continues to move toward you with unrelenting and empowering grace. He delights in meeting your needs. He finds joy in bringing peace and hope to your heart. He really is everything that you need. Why would you run anywhere else in your time of weakness or trouble?

FOR FURTHER STUDY AND ENCOURAGEMENT
Isaiah 12

DAY 16

*Why do we say we place our hope in the cross
of the Lord Jesus Christ and yet practically ask the
law to do what only grace can accomplish?*

IT'S DONE EVERY DAY IN Christian homes around the world.
Well-meaning parents, zealous to see their children doing what
is right, ask the law to do in the lives of their children what
only grace can accomplish. They think that if they have the
right set of rules, the right threat of punishment, and consistent
enforcement, their children will be okay. In ways these parents
fail to understand, they have reduced parenting to being a law-
giver, a prosecutor, a jury, and a jailer. They think that their
job is to do anything they can to shape, control, and regulate
the behavior of their children. And in their zeal to control
behavior, they look to the tools of threat ("I'll make you afraid
enough that you'll never do this again."), manipulation ("I'll
find something you really want and tell you that I'll give it
to you if you obey."), and guilt ("I'll make you feel so bad, so
ashamed, that you'll decide to not do this again.").

This way of thinking denies two significant things that the
Bible tells us. The first is that before sin is a matter of behavior,
it is always a matter of the heart. We sin because we are sinners.
For example, anger is always an issue of the heart before it is
an act of physical aggression. This is important to recognize
because no human being has the power to change the heart of
another human being. The second is that if threats, manipula-

tion, and guilt could create lasting change in the life of another person, Jesus would not have had to come. So this way of thinking denies the gospel that we say we hold dear. It really does ask the law to do what only God in amazing grace is able to accomplish. If you deny the gospel at street level, you will attempt to create by human means what only God can create by powerful grace, and it will never lead you anywhere good.

Thankfully, God hasn't left us to our own power to change. He meets us with transforming grace and calls us to be tools of that grace in his redemptive hands. He lifts the burden of change off our shoulders and never calls us to do what only he can do. So we expose our children to God's law and faithfully exercise authority while we seek to be tools of heart change in the hands of a God whose grace is greater than all of the sin we're grappling with.

FOR FURTHER STUDY AND ENCOURAGEMENT
Romans 5:12–21

DAY 17

If you hook the hope of your heart to the people
around you, you will always be disappointed.
No one is able to be your personal messiah.

YOU SHOULD BE THANKFUL for the people whom God places
in your life. You should love them dearly. You should treat
them with honor and respect. You should do all you can to
maintain the unity and peace of your relationships with them.
You should be willing to give to and serve them. You should be
open to them as they speak into your life. You should recognize that you were designed to live in loving community with
others like them. But you cannot look to them to provide for
you what only God can provide.

There are many, many Christian relationships that are hurt-
ful, painful, and marked by conflict and disappointment because the people in those relationships are placing a burden
on those relationships that no human relationship can bear.

- No person can be the source of your identity.
- No one can be the basis of your happiness.
- No individual can give you a reason to get up in the
  morning and continue.
- No loved one can be the carrier of your hope.
- No one is able to change you from the inside out.
- No human being can alter your past.
- No person is able to atone for your wrongs.
- No one can give your heart peace and rest.

Asking another human being to do those things is like requiring him to be the fourth member of the Trinity and then judging him when he falls short. It simply cannot and will not work. You see, it is vital to remember that human love is a wonderful thing, but you will only ever find life—real, heart-changing, soul-satisfying life—in a vertical relationship. You should enjoy human love, but you should look to God for your spiritual vitality and strength. You should commit to long-term, loving, mutually serving relationships, but you must remember that only God can save you, change you, and deliver you from you. You should be willing to make sacrifices of love for others, but you should place your hope only in the once-for-all sacrifice of the Lord Jesus Christ.

Could it be that the disappointment you experience in your relationships is the product of unrealistic and unattainable expectations? Could it be that you have unwittingly put people in God's place? Could it be that you ask the person next to you to do for you what only God can do? There is but one Savior, and he is yours forever. You don't need to put that burden on the person next to you.

FOR FURTHER STUDY AND ENCOURAGEMENT
2 Timothy 4:9–18

DAY 18

*God will not rest from his redemptive work until he has
once and for all presided over the funeral of sin and death.*

IF SOMEONE ASKED YOU, "What is God doing right now?" what
would you answer? I am afraid that many of us are confused
when it comes to the present benefits and activity of Jesus.
We get that we have been forgiven and we understand that we
have eternity with him in our future, but we're not sure what
the agenda is in the here and now. Because we don't understand what God has committed himself to in the present, we
are tempted to question his wisdom and doubt his love. Our
problem is not that God is inactive or that he has abandoned
us, but that we are not on his agenda page. Left with confusion
about his plan and carrying with us unrealistic expectations, we
get disappointed and a little bit cynical, and we quit running
to him for help. It is a bit of a spiritual mess.

The answer to the big question we have proposed is really
quite easy and straightforward. What is God up to right here,
right now? Redemption! He is actively working on sin's final
defeat and our complete deliverance. He is working out the
spoils of the victory that Christ accomplished on the cross of
Calvary. Listen to the encouraging words of 1 Corinthians
15:25–26: "For he must reign until he has put all his enemies
under his feet. The last enemy to be destroyed is death."

Now, you and I need to understand two things in these
words that answer our question. What is God doing? First,

he's reigning! No, your world is not out of control. No, the bad guys are not going to win. No, sin will not have the final victory. Because your world is not out of control but under God's careful redemptive control, you can have hope even when it looks to you as if darkness is winning the day.

What is God doing? This passage gives a second answer. He is putting the enemies of his redemptive purpose under his feet. He will crush enemy after enemy until the last enemy, death, is defeated. He will not sit down, he will not rest, he will not relent until sin and death are completely defeated and we are finally and forever delivered. Hope right here, right now doesn't rest in your understanding or strength, but in the sin- and death-defeating rule of the King of kings and Lord of lords. His reign is your present protection and your future hope.

FOR FURTHER STUDY AND ENCOURAGEMENT
1 Corinthians 15:50–58

DAY 19

*Could there be a greater consolation known
to man than these six hope-giving words:
"His mercies are new every morning"?*

POST THOSE SIX WORDS on the mirror that you look into each morning. Affix them on the door of your refrigerator. Tape them to the dashboard of your car. Glue them on the inside of your glasses. Put them somewhere where you will see them every day. Don't allow yourself to have a view of yourself, of others, of circumstances, of daily joys and struggles, of God, of meaning and purpose, and of what life is all about that is devoid of this gorgeous redemptive reality: mercy.

Mercy is the theme of God's story. Mercy is the thread that runs through all of Scripture. Mercy is the reason for Jesus's coming. Mercy is what your desperate heart needs. Mercy is the healer your relationships need. Mercy is what gives you comfort in weakness and hope in times of trial. Mercy can do what the law is powerless to do. Mercy not only meets you in your struggle, but guarantees that someday your struggle will end. Mercy is what this sin-broken world groans for. Mercy triumphs where justice can't. If God offered us only justice, no one would run to him. It is the knowledge of his mercy that makes us honestly face ourselves and gladly run to him. And it is mercy that we will sing about and celebrate a million years into eternity.

I love the words of Lamentations 3:22–23: "The steadfast love of the LORD never ceases; his mercies never come to an end; they are new every morning; great is your faithfulness." Let these amazing words sink in. If you are God's child, they describe your identity and your hope. They give you reason to get up in the morning and to continue. They enable you to face and admit how messed up you really are. They allow you to extend mercy to the failing people around you. And they allow you to be comforted by God's presence rather than be terrified at the thought that he is near.

Not only does God lavish on you love that will never cease and grace that will never end, and not only is he great in faithfulness, but the mercy he extends to you and to me is renewed each new morning. It is not tired, stale, irrelevant, worn out, ill-fitting, yesterday mercy. No, God's mercy is *new morning mercy*. It is formfitted for the needs of your day. It is sculpted to the shape of the weaknesses, circumstances, and struggles of each and every one of his children. Yes, we all get the same mercy, but it doesn't come to all of us in the same size and shape. God knows who you are, where you are, and what you're facing, and in the majestic combination of divine knowledge, power, and compassion, he meets you with just the right mercies for the moment. Stop allowing yourself to assess your life in a way that is devoid of new morning mercies. Any scan of your life that doesn't include those mercies is tragically lacking in truth.

FOR FURTHER STUDY AND ENCOURAGEMENT

Daniel 9:4–19

DAY 20

Living in this present broken world is designed by
God to produce longing, readiness, and hope in me.

IT'S NOT NATURAL FOR US to think about our lives in this way, but the difficulties we all face in this broken world are not in the way of God's plan. No, they are part of it. The fallen world that is your address is not your address because he didn't think through his redemptive plan very well. You are living where you're living and facing what you're facing because that's exactly how God wanted it to be. The hardships that we all face between the "already" and the "not yet" are not a sign of the failure of God's redeeming work, but rather a very important tool of it.

What we are all going through right here, right now is a massive, progressive process of values clarification and heart protection. God is daily employing the brokenness of this present world to clarify your values. Why do you need this? You need it because you struggle in this life to remember what is truly important, that is, what God says is important. You and I place much more importance on things than they truly possess, and when we do so, these things begin to claim our heart allegiance. So God ordains for us to experience that physical things get old and break. The people in our lives fail us. Relationships sour and become painful. Our physical bodies weaken. Flowers die and food spoils. All of this is meant to teach us that these things are beautiful and enjoyable, but they cannot give us what we all long for—life.

In this world that is groaning, God is protecting our hearts. He is protecting us from us. Our hearts can be so fickle. We can worship God one day, only to turn and give the worship of our hearts to something else the next. So, in love, God lets pieces of the creation die in our hands so that increasingly we are freed from asking earth to give us what only he can give. He works through loss to protect us from giving our allegiance to things that will never, ever deliver what our hearts seek. This is all designed to deepen our love and worship of him. It is all crafted to propel the joy that we have in him. And in so doing, he is preparing us for that moment when we will be freed from this present travail and give all of our being to the worship of him forever and ever.

Your Lord knows that even though you are his child, your heart is still prone to wander, so in tender, patient grace he keeps you in a world that teaches you that he alone is worthy of the deepest, most worshipful allegiance of your heart.

FOR FURTHER STUDY AND ENCOURAGEMENT
1 Peter 1:3–12

DAY 21

*If God is your Father, the Son is your Savior,
and the Spirit is your indwelling Helper, you
have hope no matter what you're facing.*

WHO IN THE WORLD DO YOU think you are? I'm serious. Who do you think you are? You and I are always assigning to ourselves some kind of identity. And the things that you and I do are shaped by the identity that we have given ourselves. So it's important to acknowledge that God has not just forgiven you (and that is a wonderful thing), but he has also given you a brand-new identity. If you're God's child, you are now a son or daughter of the King of kings and the Lord of lords. You are in the family of the Savior, who is your friend and brother. You are the temple where the Spirit of God now lives. Yes, it really is true—you've been given a radically new identity.

The problem, sadly, is that many of us live in a constant, or at least a rather regular, state of *identity amnesia*. We forget who we are, and when we do, we begin to give way to doubt, fear, and timidity. Identity amnesia makes you feel poor when in fact you are rich. It makes you feel foolish when in fact you are in a personal relationship with the one who is wisdom. It makes you feel unable when in fact you have been blessed with strength. It makes you feel alone when in fact, since the Spirit lives inside of you, it is impossible for you to be alone. You feel unloved when in fact, as a child of the heavenly Father, you have been graced with eternal love. You feel like you don't measure up when in fact the Savior measured up on your behalf. Identity amnesia sucks the life out of your Christianity in the right here, right now moment in which all of us live.

If you've forgotten who you are in Christ, what are you left with? You're left with *Christless Christianity*, which is little more than a system of theology and rules. And you know that if all you needed was theology and rules, Jesus wouldn't have had to come. All God would have needed to do was drop the Bible down on you and walk away. But he didn't walk away; he invaded your life as Father, Savior, and Helper. By grace, he made you a part of his family. By grace, he made you the place where he lives. And he did all this so that you not only would receive his forgiveness, but so that you would have everything you need for life and godliness.

So if you're his child, ward off the fear that knocks on your door by remembering who God is and who you've become as his chosen child. And don't just celebrate his grace; let it reshape the way you live today and the tomorrows that follow.

FOR FURTHER STUDY AND ENCOURAGEMENT

1 John 3:1–10

DAY 22

*It's never hopeless and you're never helpless if Immanuel
has invaded your life with his glory and grace.*

IT IS A REMARKABLE STORY, recorded for our insight, remembrance, and encouragement. It's a window on what every believer needs and has been given by God's grace:

> Now Jericho was shut up inside and outside because of the people of Israel. None went out, and none came in. And the LORD said to Joshua, "See, I have given Jericho into your hand, with its king and mighty men of valor. You shall march around the city, all the men of war going around the city once. Thus shall you do for six days. Seven priests shall bear seven trumpets of rams' horns before the ark. On the seventh day you shall march around the city seven times, and the priests shall blow the trumpets. And when they make a long blast with the ram's horn, when you hear the sound of the trumpet, then all the people shall shout with a great shout, and the wall of the city will fall down flat, and the people shall go up, everyone straight before him." So Joshua the son of Nun called the priests and said to them, "Take up the ark of the covenant and let seven priests bear seven trumpets of rams' horns before the ark of the LORD." And he said to the people, "Go forward. March around the city and let the armed men pass on before the ark of the LORD." (Josh. 6:1–7)

The children of Israel had entered the promised land, but lest they forget who they were and what they had been given, God put a trial in front of them that would powerfully demonstrate his glory and grace, which he was willing to exercise for their salvation. There was no way that this ragtag group of pilgrims would ever be able to defeat the fortified city of Jericho, but that was precisely the point. So God asked them to march around the city one time a day for six days, and then, on the seventh day, to parade around it seven times. Now, from a human perspective, what God was proposing was military suicide. God was teaching Israel that they must no longer look at life from the vantage point of human wisdom and strength because they were now the children of the Lord almighty. Their world of weakness and limits had been invaded by one of awesome grace and glory. As they walked around Jericho, God was confronting Israel with their inability, vulnerability, and dependency, and comforting them with the reality that he would be with them wherever they went and whatever they faced. They would face no enemies on their own. They would carry no needs by themselves. They would not have to bear the burden or carry their destiny in their own hands. Grace and glory had come to them in the presence of the Lord, and in the power of the Lord the walls would come down.

If you're God's child, you too must remember who you are and what you've been given. It is never you against the world, because your life has been invaded by the grace and glory of Immanuel. Say no to fear and live with the hope and courage that come only when you remember that the Lord is near.

FOR FURTHER STUDY AND ENCOURAGEMENT
Hebrews 13:1–6

DAY 23

As God's child, you don't sit and wait for hope. No, grace makes it possible for you to get up and live in hope.

GOSPEL HOPE IS A MOUTHFUL. It includes so many wonderful provisions that it's hard to get it all in one bite. Yes, biblical hope gives you a lot of spiritual nutrients to chew on. Yet many believers seem to live hope-deprived lives. Perhaps one of the dirty secrets of the church is how much we do out of fear and not faith. We permit ourselves to feel small, unable, alone, unprepared, and bereft of resources. We tell ourselves that what we're facing is too big and requires too much of us. We stand at the bottom of mountains of trouble and give up before we've taken the first step of the climb. We wait for hope to come in some noticeable, seeable way, but it never seems to arrive. We pray, but it doesn't seem to do any good. We want to believe that God is there and that he really does care, but it seems that we've been left to ourselves. With each passing day, it seems harder to have hope for our marriages, for our children, for our churches, for our friendships, or just for the ability to survive all the trouble with our faith and sanity intact. We wonder, "Where is hope to be found?"

What we fail to understand is that we don't have a hope problem; we have a sight problem. Hope has come. "What?" you say. "Where?" Hope isn't a thing. Hope isn't a set of circumstances. Hope isn't first a set of ideas. As we have already seen, hope is a person, and his name is Jesus. He came to earth to face what you face and to defeat what defeats you so that you would have hope. Your salvation means that you are now in a personal relationship with the one who is hope. You have hope because he exists and is your Savior. You don't have a hope problem; you have been given hope that is both real and constant. The issue is whether you see it. Paul captures the problem this way in Ephesians 1:18–19: ". . . having the *eyes of your hearts* enlightened, that you may know what is the hope to which he has called you, what are the riches of his glorious inheritance in the saints, and what is the immeasurable greatness of his power toward us who believe, according to the working of his great might."

Paul prays that we will have a well-working spiritual vision system so that we will "see" the hope that we have been given in Christ. What is this hope? It is a rich inheritance. Jesus died and left us a rich inheritance of grace to be invested in facing the troubles of the here and now. It is great power that is ours in the moments when we are so weak. Hope came, and he brought with him riches and power that he gave to you. You see, you don't really have a hope problem; you have a vision problem, and for that there's enlightening grace.

FOR FURTHER STUDY AND ENCOURAGEMENT
Ephesians 2:11–22

DAY 24

Hopelessness is the doorway to hope. You have to give up on yourself before you will be excited about the hope that is yours in Christ Jesus.

WE TEND TO GIVE OURSELVES far too much credit:

- We tend to attribute too much righteousness to ourselves.
- We tend to think we have more wisdom than we do.
- We tend to pride ourselves on having the "right" character.
- We tend to think of ourselves as being more patient than we are.
- We tend to regard ourselves as perseverant.
- We tend to think we are submissive and obedient.
- We tend to believe we are more committed to the kingdom of God than we are.
- We simply tend to see ourselves as more godly than we are.

Here's the problem with this tendency: when you name yourself as righteous, when you attribute to yourself more maturity than you actually have, you don't seek the grace that is your only hope. We don't think we devalue grace, but that's exactly what many of us do. Because we look at ourselves and conclude that we're spiritually okay, we don't tend to have a deep esteem and appreciation for the grace that is our only hope in life and in death. You see, only people who acknowledge how deep their need is and who admit that they have no ability whatsoever to meet that need on their own get excited about the grace that meets every one of their spiritual needs.

On the other hand, we don't like to think of ourselves as needy, so we tend to minimize our sin. Sadly, many of us are far more concerned about the sin of others than our own. We pay far more attention to the spiritual needs of others than our own. Because we minimize our sin, seeing ourselves as righteous, we don't cry out for and run after the rescuing and transforming grace that is ours as the children of God. As long as we still have hope in us—that is, hope in our ability to be righteous on our own—we won't run after the grace that is offered us in Christ Jesus. It's only when we are willing to give up on us that we seek the rescue that God offers us.

Yes, it really is true that hopelessness is the doorway to hope. Seeing yourself as hopeless and helpless if left to yourself initiates and ignites your pursuit of God's grace. The fact is that we all give daily evidence of our continuing need for grace. Simply put, we have no ability to make it on our own. We still stand in desperate need of divine help. Are you willing to admit that and run to where grace can be found?

FOR FURTHER STUDY AND ENCOURAGEMENT
Hebrews 4:14–16

DAY 25

The good life is not found in the success of my will,
but in the submission of all things to God's will.

IT WAS A 1950S TELEVISION program unlike anything that
would be broadcast today. Even its title is politically incorrect in today's culture (despite this, its episodes are still being
aired). *Father Knows Best* was the says-it-all title of this iconic
TV series. Maybe today the program would be called *Everyone
but Father Knows Best*.

Perhaps *Father Knows Best* is not such a bad title for the
section of the Lord's Prayer that says, "Your will be done . . ."
(Matt. 6:10b). Here's what we all need to keep in mind at all
times: the one who rules over this world is the ultimate definition of everything that is good, wise, right, loving, faithful, and
true. Hope in life is never about doing whatever you need to
do to get your way. Hope in life is not found in expending all
your resources, time, energy, and gifts to realize your personal
dreams. Hope in life is not found in working yourself into
as much control as possible over the people and situations in
your life. In a word, hope is not found in your will being done.

Hope is found in only one place—in the wise and faithful
rule of your Father in heaven. With his "before origin to beyond
destiny" perspective, he really does know what is best for you
and for everything he created. Prayer is never about asking God
to submit his awesome power to your will and plan; prayer is
an act of personal submission to the always-right will of God.

Now, here's the problem—we all go through times in our lives when we slide into thinking that we're smarter than God, that is, that what we want for ourselves is better than what he wants for us. We chafe against what he has put on our plates. We rebel against how he has told us to live in his word. We wonder why our lives seem harder than those of the people next to us. We wonder why breaking one of God's little laws to make things better is such a bad thing.

So cry out for grace. The war between God's will and your will has not yet ended. The desire for God to exercise his power to deliver your personal dreams is not yet gone. The temptation to think that you know better still has the power to capture you. Reach out for the help your Savior died to give you. Ask him again to rescue you from you. Pray for the sense of heart to know that there is no safer place to be than in submission to the will of your Father in heaven. And have the courage this morning to look toward heaven and say, "Your kingdom come, your will be done right here, right now in my life as it is in heaven." And thank God that he cared for you so much that he exercised his will for your welfare and salvation. When you're joyfully willing to submit to the will of the Father, you know grace has taken residence in your heart.

FOR FURTHER STUDY AND ENCOURAGEMENT
Isaiah 26

DAY 26

*No, you don't know what you'll face today, but
your sovereign Savior does, and his mercies are
new and formfitted for what you will face.*

THEY ARE GLORIOUSLY COMFORTING WORDS, the kinds of words that need to live fresh in the minds of all of God's children this side of eternity. Listen to Hebrews 4:14–16:

> Since then we have a great high priest who has passed through the heavens, Jesus, the Son of God, let us hold fast our confession. For we do not have a high priest who is unable to sympathize with our weaknesses, but one who in every respect has been tempted as we are, yet without sin. Let us then with confidence draw near to the throne of grace, that we may receive mercy and find grace to help in time of need.

Consider the hope that is built into these words:

We have a high priest. If all this passage said were this, it would be amazing. The fact that Jesus sits now at the Father's right hand and makes constant intercession for us is a redemptive miracle worthy of eternal celebration.

Our high priest sympathizes with our weaknesses. But there is more. This high priest is uniquely able to be touched by the weakness of our human condition. He is not cold or indifferent to our struggles in any way.

We run to a high priest who has been through what we've been through and more. It is comforting to remember that this one is so easily touched by our struggles because he walked in our shoes. He willingly faced all that we face and more. He faced higher and deeper pressures than we do, but he never broke, whereas we all give in somewhere along the way.

We can go to him with confidence. The result of all of this is that in our struggles with weakness within and temptation without, we have someone we can turn to with complete confidence and sure hope. He really does hold in his hands everything that we need.

We can expect mercy that is formfitted for our particular needs. Because of his grace, what can we expect? On the basis of his faithful presence and his reliable promises, we can expect mercies exactly right for what we are now facing, and nothing less.

When you struggle and are confronted with your weakness, say to yourself, "For this I have a reliable and understanding high priest."

FOR FURTHER STUDY AND ENCOURAGEMENT
Hebrews 1

DAY 27

*God's grace calls you to suffer and it calls you
to wait, but it never calls you to stand in
your own strength or to stand alone.*

THE BIBLE NEVER DENIES REALITY. The Bible never plays it safe. The Bible never offers you a cosmeticized view of the fallen world. The Bible never tricks you into thinking that things are better than they are. The Bible is straightforward and honest but not void of hope. While it is very candid about the hardships of life in this broken world, the Bible is also gloriously hopeful. The honesty does not crush the hope, but neither does the hope negate the honesty. Psalm 28 is a good example of the important harmony of these two themes:

> To you, O LORD, I call;
> > my rock, be not deaf to me,
> lest, if you be silent to me,
> > I become like those who go down to the pit.
> Hear the voice of my pleas for mercy,
> > when I cry to you for help,
> when I lift up my hands
> > toward your most holy sanctuary.
>
> Do not drag me off with the wicked,
> > with the workers of evil,
> who speak peace with their neighbors
> > while evil is in their hearts.

Give to them according to their work
    and according to the evil of their deeds;
give to them according to the work of their hands;
    render them their due reward.
Because they do not regard the works of the LORD
    or the work of his hands,
he will tear them down and build them up no more.

Blessed be the LORD!
    For he has heard the voice of my pleas for mercy.
The LORD is my strength and my shield;
    in him my heart trusts, and I am helped;
my heart exults,
    and with my song I give thanks to him.

The LORD is the strength of his people;
    he is the saving refuge of his anointed.
Oh, save your people and bless your heritage!
    Be their shepherd and carry them forever."

This psalm of trouble ends up being a psalm of shining hope. That's the story of the life of every believer, because you and I are never alone in our trouble. The "saving refuge" is always with us!

FOR FURTHER STUDY AND ENCOURAGEMENT
Psalm 35

DAY 28

Since by grace God forgives, it makes no
sense to hide, excuse, or shift the blame
when you are faced with your sin.

HERE'S THE BOTTOM LINE WHEN it comes to moral candor—
denial is rooted in fear and confession is rooted in hope. You
cannot embrace the radical hope of the person and work of the
Lord Jesus Christ and make sense out of our drive to present
ourselves as less than needy. But that instinct is alive and well in
many of us. When faced with our sin, we immediately excuse
ourselves or shift the blame. When our consciences bother us,
we hide the wrong that we have done like Adam and Eve hiding from God in the garden, or we try to convince ourselves
that what we did was not so bad after all.

Now, because God's world is so big, there will always be
places to hide, and because you live in a world that doesn't
operate as God intended, there will always be people and things
to blame, but it is all one big, sad, irrational lie. Why would
you and I work so hard to hide or deny what has been fully,
completely, and eternally forgiven? Why would we work so
hard to pretend that we are something less than sinners when
the message of the gospel is that Jesus loves and accepts sinners? Why would we hide in guilt when Jesus has fully borne
our guilt? Why would we allow ourselves to be motivated by
shame when Jesus willingly carried our shame? Why would we
construct a false façade of righteousness when Jesus has given

his righteousness over to our account? Why would we fear God's wrath when Jesus took the full brunt of God's anger for us on the cross? Why would we care what others will think of us if we're honest about our sin when the one who holds our destiny in his hands has accepted us as if we had never sinned? Why deny who we are and what we need when full provision has been made? Why act as if we're something that we're not when grace has met us right where we are? Why act as if no one would understand when we have been given a faithful and understanding high priest who is sympathetic with all our weaknesses? Why act as if there is no hope for people like us when our Savior has conquered sin and death for us? Why sing the truths of the gospel on Sunday and functionally deny the gospel during the week in street-level acts of denial, excusing, and blame? Why would you defend yourself when a loved one points out a wrong or excuse yourself when you are caught? Why, in the face of wrong, would you work to soften the pain of conviction by debating the Holy Spirit's gracious prompting?

Paul encouraged the believers in Colossae to "continue in the faith, stable and steadfast, not shifting from the hope of the gospel that you heard" (Col. 1:23). Forsake excusing, denial, and all other acts of gospel irrationality that minimize your sin. That way, you will never forget the awesome hope that you have been given in Jesus.

FOR FURTHER STUDY AND ENCOURAGEMENT
Philippians 3:1–11

DAY 29

You have not been left to secure your own future,
because God in grace has secured an end to your
story more glorious than you can grasp.

YOU AND I ABSOLUTELY NEED our lives to be shaped and re-shaped by these words:

> Blessed be the God and Father of our Lord Jesus Christ! According to his great mercy, he has caused us to be born again to a living hope through the resurrection of Jesus Christ from the dead, to an inheritance that is imperishable, undefiled, and unfading, kept in heaven for you, who by God's power are being guarded through faith for a salvation ready to be revealed in the last time. (1 Pet. 1:3–5)

One of the most common human fears is fear of the future. We all ask, "What will happen if . . . ?" or "What will happen next?" or "What is down the road?" Embedded in all of this is the hope that we will be secure and things will be all right in the future. It is not insane to wonder about the future. It is not a sin to be concerned about what is to come. It is not wrong to plan for the future. In fact, you and I should live with the future in view every day of our lives. In some ways, everything that we think, desire, decide, do, and say should be shaped by what is to come. But there is a huge difference between worrying about what you have no power over and resting in what God has revealed about his future plans for you.

Peace and hope are never to be found in your efforts to figure out the future. God's secret will is called his secret will precisely because it is secret! No, real hope is found in living inside the implications of what it means that God holds your future in his wise, powerful, and gracious hands. Peter says, "Don't ever let yourself forget that Jesus has purchased a future for you that is better than anything you could have dreamed of or planned for yourself." If you remember that you have this wonderful future ahead of you, you won't live as if this moment is all you have and you will be free of the anxiety of fearing that somehow this moment will pass you by. I love the qualifying words that Peter uses to describe our inheritance as the children of God: "imperishable, undefiled, and unfading." Together they mean that this inheritance is protected and untouchable; nothing will be allowed to happen that would damage it in any way. It is absolutely secure.

But Peter says more. He says that not only is God keeping your inheritance, he's keeping you. He's not only protecting what is to come, he's protecting you, so that when what is to come has come, you will be there to receive it and enjoy it forever and ever. So remember today that no matter how hard your story is right here, right now, it is guaranteed for you as God's child that it will end better than anything you can now imagine, and that glory will never end!

FOR FURTHER STUDY AND ENCOURAGEMENT
1 Thessalonians 4:13–5:11

DAY 30

*Jesus willingly lived without an earthly home
so that by grace we would be guaranteed a
place in the Father's home forever.*

IT IS AN AMAZING STORY, one that becomes no less amazing with every retelling. The King of kings and Lord of lords leaves the splendor of glory to come to a shattered earth to suffer and die for self-oriented rebels. The Messiah is not born in a palace, but in a stable. He lives his life as a pilgrim, denied a small luxury even animals enjoy—a home (Matt. 8:20). He is despised and rejected, then subjected to a bloody and painful public crucifixion. And he does it all intentionally and willingly so that those rebels will be forgiven, so that those separated from God will have a home with him forever, and so that grace will be supplied to people in desperate need of it.

The words of the wonderful old Christmas hymn "Thou Didst Leave Thy Throne" capture so well the stunning contrast between Jesus's suffering and our resultant blessing:

Thou didst leave Thy throne and Thy kingly crown,
When Thou camest to earth for me;
But in Bethlehem's home was there found no room
For Thy holy nativity.

Heaven's arches rang when the angels sang,
Proclaiming Thy royal degree;

But of lowly birth didst Thou come to earth,
And in great humility.

The foxes found rest, and the birds their nest
In the shade of the forest tree;
But Thy couch was the sod, O Thou Son of God,
In the deserts of Galilee.

Thou camest, O Lord, with the living Word,
That should set Thy people free;
But with mocking scorn and with crown of thorn,
They bore Thee to Calvary.

When the heav'ns shall ring, and her choirs shall sing,
At Thy coming to victory,
Let Thy voice call me home, saying "Yet there is room,
There is room at My side for thee."

Not just at Christmas but throughout the year, remember that you have an eternal home, because in amazing grace Jesus was willing to leave his home and have no home.

FOR FURTHER STUDY AND ENCOURAGEMENT
Luke 9:57–62

DAY 31

Where is hope to be found? In five life-altering words: "I am with you always."

YOU AND I ARE ON A CONSTANT quest for hope. We all want a reason to get up in the morning and motivation to continue. Here are some things you have to know about hope:

God hardwired human beings for hope. We don't live by instinct; we all find our identity, meaning, purpose, and inner sense of well-being in something.

What you place your hope in will set the direction of your life. Whether you know it or not, your life path is directed by hope. Whether it's hope in a philosophy, a person, a dream, a location, or whatever, your life will be shaped by what you place your hope in.

Hope always includes an expectation *and an* object. I am hoping for something and hoping that someone or something will deliver it.

Hope, to be hope, has to fix what is broken. Hope that does not address your needs isn't very hopeful. You place your hope in your mechanic only if he has the ability to fix what's broken in your car.

You always preach to yourself a gospel of some kind of hope. You're always reaching for hope and preaching to yourself the validity of what you reach for.

But here is the radical truth of the gospel. Hope is not a situation. Hope is not a location. Hope is not a possession. Hope is not an experience. Hope is more than an insight or a truism. As I've said before, hope is a person, and his name is Jesus! He comes to you and makes a commitment of hope: "And behold, I am with you always, to the end of the age" (Matt. 28:20). Now, there's hope. You have something profoundly deeper to hold on to than the hope that people will be nice to you, that your job will work out, that you will make good choices when tempted, that you'll be smart enough to make good decisions, that you'll be able to avoid poverty or sickness, or that you'll have a good place to live and enough to eat. No, this is eternal and deeply personal hope. It rests in the truth that Jesus has wrapped his powerful arms around you and he will never, ever let you go. If nothing you envisioned ever works out and all the bad things that you've dreaded come your way, you still have hope, because he is with you in power and grace.

FOR FURTHER STUDY AND ENCOURAGEMENT
Haggai 1:12–15

DAY 32

*The gift of eternal life guarantees that I have
been and will be forgiven, and that every broken
thing inside me will be completely repaired.*

IT REALLY IS LOCATION, LOCATION, LOCATION. If you're going to live with peace of heart and with hope and courage, you have to know your place in the work of God. There are two markers of that work that really do locate you, tell you what God is doing, and inform you as to how you should live right here, right now. As I have said before, you live between the "already" and the "not yet."

First, it is vital for you and me to always remember that we live in the "already" of *complete forgiveness.* Forgiveness is not a "hope it will be" thing. It's an "accomplished and done" thing. You do not have to hope that you will be forgiven. You do not have to be concerned that the process of forgiveness will somehow fail. Why? Because your complete and final forgiveness was accomplished on the cross of Jesus Christ. The perfect sacrifice of the completely righteous Lamb fully satisfied the holy requirements of God and left you righteous and without penalty in his sight. So you never have to worry that you will be so bad that God will reject you. You never have to hide your sin. You never have to do things to win God's favor. You never have to cower in shame. You never have to rationalize, excuse, defend, or shift the blame. You never have to pretend that you are better than you are. You never have to present arguments for your righteousness. You never have to fear being known or exposed. You never have to compare the size of your sin to the size of another's. You never have to parade your righteousness so it can be seen by others. You never have to wonder if God's going to get exhausted with how often you mess up. All of these are acts of gospel irrationality because you have been completely forgiven.

On the other end, it is essential to understand the "not yet" of your *final repair*. Yes, you have been fully forgiven, but you have not yet been completely rebuilt into all that grace will make you. Sin still remains, the war for your heart still rages, the world around you is still broken, spiritual danger still lurks, and you have not yet been fully re-formed into the image of the Lord Jesus Christ. The cross of Jesus guarantees that all of these broken things will be fixed, but they are not fixed yet.

So as I bask in the complete forgiveness that I have been given and enjoy freedom from the anxiety that I will not measure up, I cannot live unwisely. One danger (sin) still lives inside me and another (temptation) still lurks outside me, so I am still a person in daily and desperate need of grace. Forgiveness is complete. Final restoration is yet to come. Knowing you live in between the two is the key to a restful and wise Christian life.

FOR FURTHER STUDY AND ENCOURAGEMENT
2 Peter 3:1–13

DAY 33

*When we ask the present to give us what only
eternity can give, we end up driven, frustrated,
discouraged, and ultimately hopeless.*

IT'S A CASE OF MODERN evangelical schizophrenia. It causes us
so much confusion, frustration, and discouragement. It leaves
us with unrealistic expectations, naïveté toward temptation,
and regular disappointment. It leads us to ask far too much
from the people around us and to expect more than we should
from the situations and locations in our lives. It makes us search
over and over again for what we will not find and spend endless
hours wondering why we haven't found it. It even results in
some of us beginning to doubt the goodness of God.

"What is this schizophrenia?" you ask. It is the fact that we
declare that we believe in forever, yet we live as if this is all there
is. This functional contradiction between our belief system and
our daily living cannot work. Here's why.

First, you cannot make any sense out of the Christian life
without eternity. This is the whole argument of 1 Corinthians 15. If the one you've given your life to doesn't ultimately
fix all that sin has broken, so that you can live with him forever
without its effects, what is your faith worth?

Second, you and I have been hardwired for eternity. Ecclesi-
astes 3:11 declares that God has placed eternity in every person's
heart. That means everyone hungers for paradise. No one is
satisfied with things the way they are. So either you try your

hardest to turn your life right here, right now into the paradise it will never be and therefore become driven and disappointed, or you live in this broken world with the rest and peace that comes from knowing that a guaranteed place in paradise is in your future. You're sad that things are as broken as they are, so you work to be an agent of change in God's gracious and powerful hands, but you're not anxious or driven. You know that this world is not stuck and that it hasn't been abandoned by God. You know that God is working his eternal plan. He is moving things toward their final conclusion. You can't see it every day, but you know it's true. In the middle of your sadness there is celebration, because you've read the final chapter and you know how God's grand story is going to end.

So you get up every morning and give yourself to doing the things that God says are good, because you know that if grace has put eternity in your future, there's nothing that you could ever do in God's name that is in vain.

FOR FURTHER STUDY AND ENCOURAGEMENT
1 Corinthians 15:12–34

DAY 34

Without eternity in the center of our thinking, our picture of life is like a jigsaw puzzle missing a central piece.

ONE OF THE THEMES OF this devotional is that all human beings have a theological bent, whether they consider themselves religious or not. Everyone wants life to make sense. Everyone is a committed interpreter. No one leaves his or her life alone. We all pick our lives apart, trying to make sense of them. We all develop our own systems of theology, biblical or otherwise. We all develop particular philosophies of life. We all carry around with us worldviews that shape the way we think, the things that we desire, the choices that we make, the words that we say, and the actions that we take. None of us is passive. We all shape the way life looks to ourselves.

So God, knowing who we are and knowing that we are hardwired to make sense of our lives, has given us his word. In it, he reveals who he is, he defines who we are, he explains the meaning and purpose of life, he unfolds the greatest of humanity's problems—sin—and he points us to the hope of his amazing grace. He doesn't tell us everything, because we would not be able to understand everything or deal with it in our daily lives, but he does give us all the necessary pieces of an "origin-to-destiny worldview" so we can live as we were created to live.

Essential to this biblical worldview is eternity. The Bible confronts us with the reality that this is not all there is. It tells us that this world is marching toward a final conclusion. You and I are eternal beings who will spend eternity somewhere. It will either be in the presence of God forever and ever or separated from him in a place of eternal punishment forever and ever.

The reality of eternity infuses the here and now with seriousness and hope. The way you live is important because there is an eternity to follow. The choices you make are important because there is a forever. The things you believe are important because the world is moving toward eternity. The things you surrender your heart to are important because there is an eternal tomorrow. You simply cannot hold to an "all that's important is the pleasures of the moment" view of life and believe in eternity at the same time. In light of eternity, it makes no sense to forget God and live for yourself. In the face of eternity, it is irrational to write your own rules and demand your own way. Eternity requires you to take life seriously.

But eternity also fills this moment with hope. Because I know that this is not all there is, I also know that the sin, trials, and sufferings of the present will not last forever. For God's children, eternity promises that sin will die, suffering will end, our trials will be no more, and we will live with God in perfect peace forever and ever and ever. You just can't make proper sense of life without viewing it from the perspective of eternity.

FOR FURTHER STUDY AND ENCOURAGEMENT
John 5:19–29

DAY 35

*Grace works to free you from your eternity amnesia
so that you will be willing and able to live with
the purifying hope of what is to come.*

YOU AND I DON'T ALWAYS live what we say we believe. There is
often a disconnect between our confessional theology and our
street-level functional theology. There is often a separation between, on the one hand, the doctrines we say we have embraced
and, on the other hand, the choices we make and the anxieties
that we feel. One of the places where this disconnect exists for
many of us is the biblical teaching about eternity. We say we
believe in the hereafter. We say that this moment in time is
not all there is. We say that we are hardwired for forever. But
often we live with the compulsion, anxiety, and drivenness of
eternity amnesiacs. We get so focused on the opportunities,
responsibilities, needs, and desires of the here and now that
we lose sight of what is to come.

The fact is that you cannot make sense out of life un-
less you look at it from the vantage point of eternity. If
all God's grace gives us is a little better here and now, if it
doesn't finally fix all that sin had broken, then perhaps we
have believed in vain: "If in Christ we have hope in this life
only, we are of all people most to be pitied" (1 Cor. 15:19).
There has to be more to God's plan than this world of sin,
sickness, sorrow, and death. There has to be more than
the temporary pleasures of this physical world. Yes, there

is more, and when you live like there's more to come, you live in a radically different way.

When you forget eternity, you tend to lose sight of what's important. When you lose sight of what's truly important, you live for what is temporary, and your heart seeks for satisfaction where it cannot be found. Looking for satisfaction where it cannot be found leaves you spiritually empty and potentially hopeless. Meanwhile, you are dealing with all the difficulties of this fallen world with little hope that things will ever be different. Living as an eternity amnesiac just doesn't work. It leaves you either hoping that now will be the paradise it will never be or hopeless that what is broken will ever be fixed. So it's important to fix your eyes on what God has promised will surely come. Let the values of eternity be the values that shape your living today, and keep telling yourself that the difficulties of today will someday completely pass away. Belief in eternity can clarify your values and renew your hope. Pray that God, by his grace, will help you remember forever right here, right now.

FOR FURTHER STUDY AND ENCOURAGEMENT
2 Corinthians 4:7–18

DAY 36

*Of course you haven't been fulfilled in this world. It's a
sign that you have been designed for a world to come.*

IT IS AN ITEM ON each of our theological outlines, but we don't
actually live as though we believe it. We all say that we believe
that this is not all there is. We say we really do believe that
there is life after this one ends. Our formal theology contains
the fact of a new heaven and a new earth to come. But we
tend to live with the anxiety and drivenness that come when
we believe that all we have is this moment.

Here's the real-life, street-level issue: if you don't keep the
eyes of your heart focused on the paradise that is to come,
you will try to turn this poor fallen world into the paradise it
will never be. In the heart of every living person is the longing
for paradise. The cry of a toddler who has just fallen down
is a cry for paradise. The tears of the school-age child who
has been rejected on the playground are tears of one reaching
out for paradise. The pain of aloneness that a person without
friends or family feels is the pain of one longing for paradise.
The hurt the couple feels as their marriage dissolves is the
hurt of those crying out for paradise. The sadness that the old
man feels as his body weakens is the sadness of one who longs
for paradise. We all have this longing, even when we are not
aware of it, because it was placed there by our Creator. He
has placed eternity in each one of our hearts (Eccles. 3:11).
Our cries are more than cries of pain; they are also cries of

longing for more and better than we will ever experience in this fallen world.

When you forget this, you work very hard to try to turn this moment into the paradise it will never be. Your marriage will not be a paradise. Your job will not be the paradise you long for. Your friendships will not be the paradise your heart craves. The world around you will not function like paradise. Your children will not deliver paradise to you. Even your church will not live up to the standard of paradise. If you're God's child, paradise has been guaranteed for you, but it will not be right here, right now. All the things that disappoint you now are to remind you that this is not all there is and to cause you to long for the paradise that is to come. The dreams that die remind you that this is not paradise. The flowers that wilt remind you that this is not paradise. The sin that captivates you should remind you that this is not paradise. The diseases that infect you are to remind you that this is not paradise. Live in hope because paradise is surely coming, and stop asking this fallen world to be the paradise it will never be.

FOR FURTHER STUDY AND ENCOURAGEMENT
Revelation 21

DAY 37

*Corporate worship is designed to confront you
with the glory of the grace of Jesus so you won't
look for life, help, and hope elsewhere.*

AS I SAT IN THE balcony with my wife Luella, I remembered
how important and wonderful corporate worship is. It was
Tenth Presbyterian Church's Spring Choral Worship Service.
It featured the original compositions and hymn arrangements
of Robert Elmore. We were reminded in song of the miser-
able condition in which sin left us and our world, and of the
glorious rescue of redeeming grace. Each piece was so full of
the gospel that I felt as if my heart could not contain anything
more. I was thinking of the words of Psalm 89:1: "I will sing of
the steadfast love of the LORD, forever; with my mouth I will
make known your faithfulness to all generations." I thought
we could sing and sing and sing and never exhaust the stunning redemptive themes of the gospel of the Lord Jesus Christ.

Finally, after a lavish gospel meal, the crescendo anthem
came. It was such a beautiful celebration of the glory of the
gospel that when we came to the last two lines, I quit sing-
ing and began to repeat over and over again: "Amen! Amen!
Amen!" Corporate worship had performed its work in my
heart once again.

Very honestly, I hadn't come to the service with a celebra-
tory heart. I had grumbled my way into the room. It had
been a long ministry weekend. I wouldn't have gone to that

Sunday evening service if Luella hadn't begged me to. I really didn't want to be there. But in the middle of it all, something captured my heart—glory. The glory of the grace of Jesus suddenly loomed larger than the exhaustion of my body or the weariness of my mind. My cold heart was enlivened by the fire of the gospel of the grace of the Lord Jesus Christ. The talents of the musicians and the voices of the congregation reminded me once again of who I was and what I had been given in the grace of the cross of Jesus. Once again, this grumbler became a celebrant. Once again, the gathering of God's people for worship had done its job.

God ordained for us to gather for worship because he knows us and the weaknesses of our fickle, grumbling, and easily distracted hearts. He knows how soon we forget the depth of our need as sinners and the expansiveness of his provisions in Jesus Christ. He knows that little lies can deceive us and little obstacles can discourage us. He knows that self-righteousness still has the power to delude us. So in grace he calls us to gather and consider glory once again, to be excited once again, and to be rescued once again. It's not only that corporate worship reminds us of God's grace. Corporate worship is itself a gift of grace. Run with celebration to its rescue any time it is available to you.

FOR FURTHER STUDY AND ENCOURAGEMENT
Psalm 122

DAY 38

Corporate worship is designed to instill vertical
hope where horizontal hope has been dashed.

AS I'VE SAID BEFORE, every human being is hardwired for and concerned about hope. We're all in a constant search for hope that delivers and lasts. We're all a bit discouraged and paralyzed when our hopes are dashed. When one hope dies, we grab hold of another hope as fast as we can.

The Bible is a hope story. It is about hope misplaced and hope found. It's about hope that cannot deliver and hope that gives you everything that you need. It's about where not to look for hope and the only place where true hope can be found. The great hope drama of the Bible is summarized by a few very important words that are buried in the middle of the apostle Paul's letter to the Romans:

> Therefore, since we have been justified by faith, we have peace with God through our Lord Jesus Christ. Through him we have also obtained access by faith into this grace in which we stand, and we rejoice in hope of the glory of God. Not only that, but we rejoice in our sufferings, knowing that suffering produces endurance, and endurance produces character, and character produces hope, and hope does not put us to shame, because God's love has been poured into our hearts through the Holy Spirit who has been given to us. (Rom. 5:1–5)

Notice what Paul does here:

- *He connects our hope to our justification.* We have hope because, by grace, we have been forgiven and accepted by the one who holds everything we need.
- *He connects our hope to the glory of God.* Our hope is that God will complete his work, getting the glory that is his due. His glory is our good.
- *He connects our hope to our sufferings.* There is even hope in suffering because in that suffering the God who is our hope is doing good things in us and for us.
- *He says that our vertical hope (hope in God) will never put us to shame.* This means that all other forms of hope fail us in some way. Hope in created things never delivers what hope in the Creator can.
- *He connects our hope to the Holy Spirit who lives inside us.* Here is the ultimate reason that you and I have hope— God has made us the address where he lives. This means that the one who can do more than we are able to conceive of is constantly with us and constantly working on our behalf.

Now, that's hope! As you worship God with other believers and hear the truths of his word proclaimed, your hope will be rekindled.

FOR FURTHER STUDY AND ENCOURAGEMENT
Hebrews 6:9–20

DAY 39

Corporate worship reminds you that hope
is not a situation, location, idea, or thing.
Hope is a person, and his name is Jesus.

But when the goodness and loving kindness of God our Savior appeared, he saved us, not because of works done by us in righteousness, but according to his own mercy, by the washing of regeneration and renewal of the Holy Spirit, whom he poured out on us richly through Jesus Christ our Savior, so that being justified by his grace we might become heirs according to the hope of eternal life. The saying is trustworthy, and I want you to insist on these things, so that those who have believed in God may be careful to devote themselves to good works. These things are excellent and profitable for people. (Titus 3:4–8)

Everyone wants it. It's the thing that fuels what we do. It's the thing that stimulates courage and perseverance. It's what gets you through the tough times and keeps you from quitting. It's hard to be happy and hard to get up and continue when you don't have any of it. What is it? Hope, of course. As we have seen over and over again in these pages, everyone craves hope.

Now, the radical message of the Bible, captured well by the Titus passage, is that sturdy hope, hope that won't ever fail you or leave you embarrassed, is only found vertically. The horizontal situations, locations, experiences, and relationships of everyday life are dangerous places to look for hope. Why? They all fail you. First, everywhere you could look horizontally has been affected by the fall in some way. There are simply no perfectly ideal situations, no paradise locations, no completely satisfying experiences, and surely no perfect people this side of eternity. Add to this the fact that all these things are fleeting. None of them lasts. Every horizontal thing, this side of eternity, is in the process of decay. So hope that addresses your deepest needs, that gives you reason to continue no matter how hard life is, and that promises you eternal good is only ever found vertically.

Perhaps it's not enough to say that hope is found in God and his covenant promises. That surely is true, but more needs to be said. Hope really does rest on the shoulders of the one who is the fulfillment of all those covenant promises. It's not enough to say that reliable hope is hope in Jesus. The message of the Bible is more powerful and pointed than even that. Reliable hope *is* Jesus! In his life, death, and resurrection, your life is infused with hope. The grace of the cross is not just grace that forgives and accepts, but grace that also supplies you with everything you need until you are needy no more. And what does this hope produce, according to the Titus passage? It produces a brand-new way of living. Because the one who is hope has infused my life with hope, I do not have to search for hope any longer and can now give myself to a life of good works. Do you know this hope? If not, a good first step toward finding it would be to gather with other believers this Lord's Day to worship the one who is your hope. To find hope, find him.

FOR FURTHER STUDY AND ENCOURAGEMENT

Romans 5:1–11

DAY 40

*God puts you in hard moments when you cry out
for his comfort so that your heart becomes tender
to those near you who need the same comfort.*

SOMETIMES WE ARE QUICKER to judge than to comfort. This
hit me not too long ago on the streets of Philadelphia, where
I live. I walked by a young homeless person who was begging
on the street, and I immediately thought, "I wonder what
you did to get yourself here." Criticism came more quickly to
me than compassion. Hard-heartedness is more natural for us
than I think we like to admit. We're that way with our children
when we yell at them as if we're shocked that they're strug-
gling with the same things we struggled with when we were
their ages. We're that way when we look down on the parents
who can't seem to control their children in restaurants or on
those who have trouble paying their bills. It is a function of
the self-righteousness that, in some ways, still lives inside all
of us. When we have named ourselves as strong, wise, capable,
mature, and righteous, we tend to look down on those who
have not achieved what we think we have.

So God humbles us. He puts us in situations where our
weakness, foolishness, and immaturity are exposed. I remember
how I struggled with the sovereignty of God in the painful
days after my father's death. I had previously prided myself in
how well I understood and could communicate this important
doctrine, but there I was, grappling with God's plan. At street

level, my dad's story made no sense to me. I wondered what in the world God was doing. It all looked chaotic and out of control. It was humbling to admit to my struggle, but doing so caused me to be much more sensitive to and patient with others who struggle with God's rule in hard moments in their lives.

Here is how Paul captures this in 2 Corinthians 1: "Blessed be the God and Father of our Lord Jesus Christ, the Father of mercies and God of all comfort, who comforts us in all our affliction, so that we may be able to comfort those who are in any affliction, with the comfort with which we ourselves are comforted by God. . . . If we are afflicted, it is for your comfort and salvation; and if we are comforted, it is for your comfort" (vv. 3–6). The hard moments are not just for your growth in grace, but for your call to be a tool of that same grace in the life of another sufferer. In difficulty, God is softening your heart and sharpening your edges so that you may be ready to make the comfort of the invisible Father visible in the life of the weary pilgrim he has placed in your pathway. God intends for you to give away the comfort you've been given. The grace that has given you hope is meant to spill over into hope for the person next to you. What a plan!

FOR FURTHER STUDY AND ENCOURAGEMENT
2 Corinthians 1:3–11

SCRIPTURE INDEX

PAUL TRIPP MINISTRIES

Paul Tripp Ministries is a not-for-profit organization connecting the transforming power of Jesus Christ to everyday life. Hundreds of resources are freely available online, on social media, and the Paul Tripp app.

PaulTripp.com

 /pdtripp   @paultripp   @paultrippquotes

More Devotionals
from Paul David Tripp

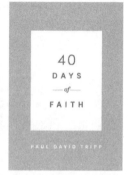

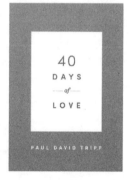

For more information, visit **crossway.org, paultripp.com,**
or anywhere Christian books are sold.